IRISH songs

IRISH songs

Selected by
Siobhan O'Brien

GEDDES &
GROSSET

Published 2002 by Geddes & Grosset David Dale House,
New Lanark, ML11 9DJ, Scotland

Selection, layout and design © 2002 Geddes & Grosset

For copyright of musical arrangements
see individual songs

Music typesetting by Chalmers Enterprises, Edinburgh

Edited by Siobhan O'Brien

All rights reserved. No part of this publication may be reproduced,
stored in a retrieval system or transmitted in any form or by
any means, electronic, mechanical, photocopying, recording or
otherwise, without the prior permission of the copyright holder

ISBN 1 84205 165 2

Printed and bound in the UK

Contents

Believe Me if All Those Endearing Young Charms	8
The Black Velvet Band	10
A Bunch of Thyme	12
Carrickfergus	14
Cockles and Mussels	17
Come Back to Erin	18
The Croppy Boy	20
The Dear Little Shamrock	22
Danny Boy (The Londonderry Air)	24
The Harp That Once Thro' Tara's Halls	26
The Garden where the Praties Grow	28
I'll Take You Home Again, Kathleen	30
I Know My Love	32
I Know Where I'm Going	34
The Irish Emigrant	36
The Irish Rover	38
An Island Spinning Song	40
Kate Kearney	42
Kitty of Coleraine	43
Kathleen Mavourneen	44
Kilgary Mountain	46
Killarney	48
The Last Rose of Summer	50
Let Erin Remember the Days of Old	51
The Low Backed Car	52

The Meeting of the Waters	54
The Minstrel Boy	56
Molly Bawn	57
Molly Brannigan	59
The Mountains of Mourne	62
Oft, in the Stilly Night	64
Rory O'More	66
The Rose of Tralee	68
She Moved Through the Fair	70
Silent, O Moyle	72
Sing, Sweet Harp	74
Slievenamon	76
The Snowy-Breasted Pearl	78
The Spinning Wheel	80
The Star of the County Down	83
Teddy O'Neale	85
There's a Heart in Old Ireland	87
The Wearin' o' the Green	89
Widow Machree	92

Believe Me if All Those Endearing Young Charms

Traditional
Words by Thomas Moore

Believe Me if All Those Endearing Young Charms

It is not while beauty and youth are thine own,
And thy cheeks unprofaned by a tear,
That the fervour and faith of a soul can be known,
To which time will but make thee more dear.
No, the heart that has truly loved never forgets
But as truly loves on to the close;
As the sunflower turns on her god, when he sets,
The same look which she turned when he rose.

The Black Velvet Band

Traditional

The Black Velvet Band

As I was walking down Broadway, not intending to stay very long,
I met with a frolicsome damsel, as she came tripping along.
A watch she pulled out of her pocket and slipped it right into my hand;
On the very first day that I met her, bad luck to the velvet band.

Her eyes they shone ...

Before the judge and the jury the both of us had to appear,
And a gentleman swore to the jewel'ry; the case against us was clear.
For seven years transportation right unto Van Dieman's Land,
Far away from my friends and relations, to follow her black velvet band.

Her eyes they shone ...

Oh, all you brave young Irish lads, a warning take by me:
Beware of the pretty young damsels that are knocking around in Tralee!
They'll treat you to whiskey and porter until you're unable to stand,
And before you have time for to leave them you are unto Van Dieman's Land.

Her eyes they shone ...

A Bunch of Thyme

Traditional

© Copyright 1997 Dorsey Brothers Music Limited, 8/9 Frith Street, London W1D 3JB.
All rights reserved. International Copyright secured. Reproduced by permission.

A Bunch of Thyme

For thyme it is a precious thing,
And thyme brings all things to my mind.
Thyme with all its labours,
Along with all its joys,
Thyme brings all things to an end.

Once she had a bunch of thyme;
She thought it never would decay.
Then came a lusty sailor
Who chanced to pass her way:
He stole her bunch of thyme away.

The sailor gave to her a rose,
A rose that never would decay.
He gave it to her
To keep her reminded
Of when he stole her thyme away.

For thyme it is a precious thing,
And thyme brings all things to my mind.
Thyme with all its labours,
Along with all its joys,
Thyme brings all things to an end.

Carrickfergus

Traditional

Carrickfergus

Carrickfergus

Now in Kilkenny it is reported,
They've got marble stones as black as ink.
With gold and silver I would transport her
But I'll sing no more now till I get a drink.
I'm drunk today but then I'm seldom sober,
A handsome rover from town to town.
Ah but I'm sick now, my days are over
Come all ye young lads and lay me down.

Cockles and Mussels

Traditional

She was a fishmonger; but sure 'twas no wonder,
For so were her father and mother before.
And they each wheeled their barrow
Thro' the streets broad and narrow
Crying "Cockles and mussels alive, alive o!"

Alive, alive o!...

She died of a fever, and no one could save her,
And that was the end of sweet Molly Malone.
Now her ghost wheels her barrow
Thro' the streets broad and narrow,
Crying "Cockles and mussels alive, alive o!"

Alive, alive o!...

Come Back to Erin

Words and music by "Claribel" (Charlotte Allington Barnard)

Come Back to Erin

Over the green sea, Mavourneen,
   Mavourneen,
Long shone the white sail that bore thee
   away,
Ridding the white waves that fair
   summer morning,
Just like a May-flower afloat on the
   bay.
Oh, but my heart sank when clouds
   came between us,
Like a grey curtain, the rain falling
   down,
Hid from my sad eyes the path o'er the
   ocean,
Far far away where my colleen had
   flown.

*Then come back to Erin, Mavourneen,
   Mavourneen...*

Oh, may the angels awaking and
   sleeping
Watch o'er my bird in the land far
   away.
And it's my prayers I'll consign to
   their keeping:
Care for my jewel by night and by
   day.
When by the fireside I watch the
   bright embers,
Then all my heart flies to England and
   thee,
Craving to know if my darling
   remembers,
Or if her thoughts may be crossing to
   me.

*Then come back to Erin, Mavourneen,
   Mavourneen...*

The Croppy Boy

Traditional

'Twas early, early in the night
The yeoman cavalry gave me a fright,
The yeoman cavalry was my downfall,
And taken was I by the Lord Cornwall.

'Twas in the guard-house where I was laid
And in the parlour where I was tried,
My sentence passed and my courage low
When to Dungannon I was forced to go.

Arrangement © 1995 International Music Publications Ltd, London W6 8BS.
Reproduced by permission. All rights reserved.

The Croppy Boy

As I was passing my father's door
My brother William stood at the door.
My aged father stood there also.
My tender mother her hair she tore.

As I was going up Wexford Street
My own first cousin I chanced to meet.
My own first cousin did me betray
And for one bare guinea swore my life away.

As I was going up Wexford Hill
Who could blame me to cry my fill?
I looked behind and I looked before.
My aged mother I shall see no more.

As I mounted on the scaffold high
My aged father was standing by.
My aged father did me deny
And the name he gave me was the Croppy Boy.

It was in Dungannon this young man died
And in Dungannon his body lies
And you good people that do pass by
Oh shed a tear for the Croppy Boy.

The Dear Little Shamrock

Words by Andrew Cherry, music by William Jackson

The Dear Little Shamrock

That dear little plant still grows in our land,
Fresh and fair as the daughters of Erin,
Whose smiles can bewitch, and whose eyes can command,
In each climate they ever appear in.
For they shine thro' the bog, thro' the brake, thro' the mire-land,
Just like their own dear little shamrock of Ireland.

The dear little shamrock, the sweet little shamrock,
The dear little, sweet little shamrock of Ireland.

That dear little plant that springs from our soil,
When its three little leaves are extended,
Denotes from the stalk we together should toil,
And ourselves by ourselves be befriended.
And still thro' the bog, thro' the brake, thro' the mire-land,
From one root should branch, like the shamrock of Ireland.

The dear little shamrock, the sweet little shamrock,
The dear little, sweet little shamrock of Ireland.

Danny Boy (The Londonderry Air)

Traditional
Words Frederick Edward Weatherly

Danny Boy

But when ye come, and all the flow'rs are dying,
If I am dead, as dead I well may be,
Ye'll come and find the place where I am lying,
And kneel and say an Ave there for me;
And I shall hear, though soft you tread above me,
And all my grave will warmer, sweeter be,
For you will bend and tell me that you love me,
And I shall sleep in peace until you come to me!

The Harp That Once Thro' Tara's Halls

Traditional
Words by Thomas Moore

The Harp That Once Thro' Tara's Halls

No more to chiefs and ladies bright
The harp of Tara swells;
The cord alone that breaks at night,
Its tale of ruin tells.
Thus freedom now so seldom wakes,
The only throb she gives
Is when some heart indignant breaks,
To show that she still lives.

The Garden where the Praties Grow

Traditional Dublin street song
Words by Johny Patterson

The Garden where the Praties Grow

She was just the sort of creature, boys,
That nature did intend,
To walk right through the world, me boys,
Without a Grecian bend.
Nor did she wear a chignon,
I'll have you all to know,
And I met her in the garden
Where the praties grow.

Says I, "My pretty Kathleen,
I'm tired of single life,
And if you've no objection, sure,
I'll make you my sweet wife."
She answered me right modestly,
And curtsied very low,
"Oh, you're welcome in the garden
Where the praties grow."

Says I, "My pretty Kathleen,
I do hope that you'll agree.'
She was not like your city girls
Who say you're making free.
Says she, "I'll ax my parents,
And tomorrow I'll let you know,
If you'll meet me in the garden
Where the praties grow."

I'll Take You Home Again, Kathleen

Words and music by Thomas P. Westendorf

I'll Take You Home Again, Kathleen

I know you love me, Kathleen, dear
Your heart was ever fond and true;
I always feel when you are near
That life holds nothing dear but you.
The smiles that once you gave to me
I scarcely ever see them now
Though many, many times I see
A darkening shadow on your brow.

Oh! I will take you back, Kathleen,
To where your heart will find no pain,
And when the fields are fresh and green
I'll take you to your home again.

To that dear home beyond the sea
My Kathleen shall again return
And when thy old friends welcome thee
Thy loving heart will cease to yearn.
Where laughs the little silver stream
Beside your master's humble cot
And brightest rays of sunshine gleam
There all your grief will be forgot.

Oh! I will take you back, Kathleen,
To where your heart will find no pain,
And when the fields are fresh and green
I'll take you to your home again.

I Know My Love

Traditional

I Know My Love

There is a dance house in Maradyke,
And there my true love goes every night.
He takes a strange one upon his knee,
And don't you know, now, that vexes me?

And still she cried, "I love him the best
"And troubled mind, sure can know no rest."
And still she cried, "Bonny boys are few,
"And if my love laves me what will I do?"

If my love knew I could wash and wring,
If my love knew I could weave and spin,
I'd make a coat of all the finest kind,
But the want of money laves me behind.

And still she cried ...

I know my love is an arrant rover,
I know he'll wander the wild world over.
In foreign parts he may chance to stray,
Where all the girls are so bright and gay.

And still she cried ...

I Know Where I'm Going

Traditional

The Irish Emigrant

Feather beds are soft,
And painted rooms are bonny;
But I would leave them all
To go with my love Johnny

Some say he's black,
But I say he's bonny,
The fairest of them all;
My handsome, winsome Johnny.

I know where I'm goin',
And I know who's goin' with me;
I know who I love,
But the dear knows who I'll marry!

The Irish Emigrant

Words by Lady Helen Dufferin, music by G Barker

The Irish Emigrant

lark's loud song is in my ear, and the corn is green a-gain, But I miss the soft clasp of your hand, and your breath warm on my cheek, And I still keep list'ning to the words, you ne-ver more may speak, You ne-ver more may speak.

I'm very lonely now, Mary; the poor make no new friends,
But oh they love the better still the few our father sends;
And you were all I had, Mary, my blessing and my pride!
There's nothing left to care for now since my poor Mary died.
I'm bidding you a long farewell, my Mary kind and true,
But I'll not forget you, darlin', in the land I'm going to.
They say there's bread and work for all, the sun shines always there,
Bur I'll ne'er forget old Ireland, were it fifty times as fair, were it fifty times as fair.

The Irish Rover

Traditional

In the year of our Lord, eight-een hun-dred and six, We set sail from the coal quay of Cork. We were sail-ing a-way with a car-go of bricks For the grand ci-ty hall in New York. We'd an e-leg-ant craft, it was rigg'd fore and aft, And how the trade winds drove her. She had twen-ty-three masts, and she stood sev-'ral blasts And they called her the I-rish Ro-ver.

Arrangement © 1995 International Music Publications Ltd, London W6 8BS.
Reproduced by permission. All rights reserved.

There was Barney Magee from the banks of the Lee,
There was Hogan from County Tyrone,
There was Johnny McGurk who was scared stiff to work
And a chap from Westmeath named Malone,
There was Slugger O'Toole who drank as a rule
And fighting Bill Tracey from Dover
And your man Mick McCann from the banks of the Bann
Was the skipper of the Irish Rover.

We had one million bags of the best Sligo rags
We had two million barrels of bone,
We had three million bales of old nanny goats' tails,
We had four million barrels of stone,
We had five million hogs and six million dogs
And seven million barrels of porter,
We had eight million sides of old horses' hides
In the hold of the Irish Rover.

We had sailed seven years when the measles broke out
And our ship lost her way in a fog
And the whole of the crew was reduced down to two:
'Twas myself and the captain's old dog,
Then the ship struck a rock, oh Lord what a shock,
And nearly tumbled over,
Turned nine times around, then the poor dog was drowned.
I'm the last of the Irish Rover.

An Island Spinning Song

Traditional

One came before her and said, beseeching, "I have fortune and I have lands, And if you will share in the goods of my household All my treasure's at your command."

An Island Spinning Song

But she said to him "the goods you proffer
Are far from my mind as the silk of the sea.
The arms of him, my young love, round me
Is all the treasure is true for me."

"Proud you are then, proud of your beauty,
But beauty's a flow'r will soon decay;
The fairest flow'rs only bloom in summer,
They bloom one summer and fade away."

My heart is sad for the little flow'r
That must soon wither where it grew,
He who has my heart in keeping
I would he had my body too.

Kate Kearney

Traditional
Words by Mrs Sydney Owenson (Lady Morgan)

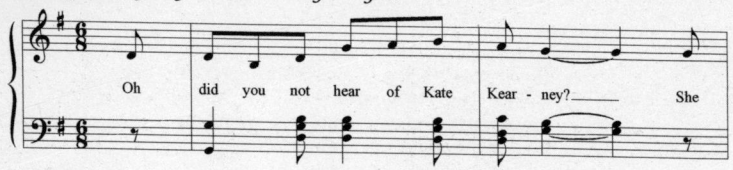

Oh did you not hear of Kate Kearney? She lives on the banks of Killarney, From the glance of her eye, Shun danger and fly, For fatal's the glance of Kate Kearney.

For that eye is so modestly beaming,
You ne'er think of mischief she's dreaming
Yet, oh! I can tell, how fatal's the spell
That lurks in the eyes of Kate Kearney.

Oh! should you e'er meet this Kate Kearney,
Who lives on the banks of Killarney
Beware of her smile, for many a wile
Lies hid in the smile of Kate Kearney.

Tho' she looks so bewitchingly simple,
Yet there's mischief in ev'ry dimple
And who dares inhale, her sigh's spicy gale
Must die by the breath of Kate Kearney.

Kitty of Coleraine

Traditional
Words by Edward Lynaught

As beau-ti-ful Kit-ty one mor-ning was trip-ping With a pit-cher of milk from the fair of Cole-raine, When she saw me she stum-bled, the pit-cher it tum-bled, And all the sweet but-ter-milk wat-er'd the plain. "Oh what shall I do now, 'twas look-ing at you now, Sure such a fine pit-cher I'll ne'er see a-gain, 'Twas the pride of my dai-ry, Oh! Bar-ney Mc-Clea-ry you're sent as a plague to the girls of Cole-raine."

I sat down beside her and gently did chide her
That such a misfortune should give her such pain;
A kiss there I gave her and before I did leave her
She vowed for such pleasure she'd break it again.

'Twas hay-making season, I can't tell the reason,
Misfortune will never come singly 'tis plain;
For very soon after poor Kitty's disaster,
Och! never a pitcher was whole in Coleraine.

Kathleen Mavourneen

Words by Mrs Julia Crawford, music by Frederick Nichols Crouch

Kath - leen Ma - vour - neen! The grey dawn is break-ing, The horn of the hun - ter is heard on the hill; The lark from her light wing the bright dew is sha - king. Kath leen Ma vour neen! what, slum - ber-ing still? Oh! hast thou for - got-ten how soon we must se - ver? Oh! hast thou for - got-ten this day we must part, It

Kathleen Mavourneen

may be for years and it may be for-ev-er, Oh! why art thou si-lent, thou voice of my heart? It may be for years and it may be for e-ver, Then why art thou si-lent, Kath-leen Ma-vour-neen?

Kathleen Mavourneen! awake from thy slumber,
The blue mountain glows in the sun's golden light;
Ah! where is the spell that once hung on thy numbers?
Arise in thy beauty, thou star of my night.
Mavourneen, Mavourneen, my sad tears are falling,
To think that from Erin and thee I must part.
It may be for years and it may be forever,
Oh! why art thou silent, thou voice of my heart?
It may be for years and it may be forever,
Then why art thou silent, Kathleen Mavourneen?

Kilgary Mountain

Traditional

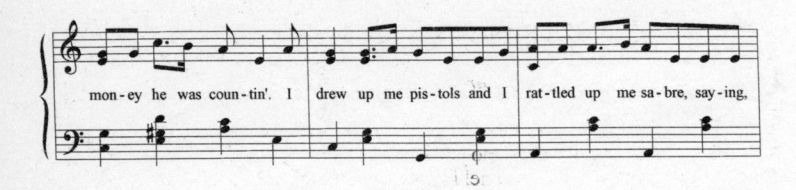

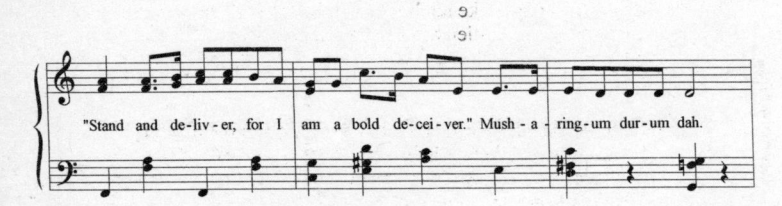

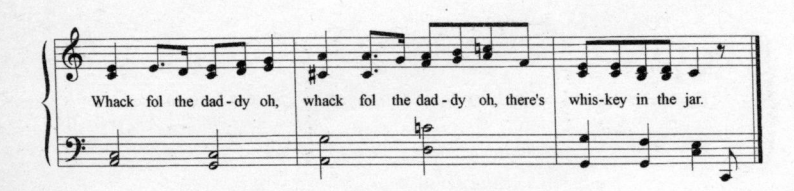

As I was a-walkin' up-on Kilgary Mountain, I met with Col'nel Pepper, and his money he was countin'. I drew up me pistols and I rattled up me sabre, saying, "Stand and deliver, for I am a bold deceiver." Mush-a-ringum durum dah. Whack fol the daddy oh, whack fol the daddy oh, there's whiskey in the jar.

The money in me hand, it looked so neat and jolly,
I took it right straight home for to give to my Molly,
She swore that she loved me and she never would
   deceive me
But the devil's in the women and they always lie so easy.
Mush-a-ring-um dur-um dah
Whack fol the daddy
Oh, whack fol the daddy
Oh, there's whiskey in the jar

Kilgary Mountain

I went to me chambers to prepare myself for slumber
To dream of gold and girls and sure it is no wonder
But Molly took me pistols and she filled them up with water
And she sent for Colonel Pepper to make ready for a slaughter.
Mush-a-ring-um dur-um dah ...

I woke next morning early, between six and seven
With guards around me bed in both numbers odd and even
I flew to me pistols, but alas I was mistaken
I couldn't shoot the water and a prisoner I was taken.
Mush-a-ring-um dur-um dah ...

They threw me into jail without a judge nor writing
For robbing Colonel Pepper up on Kilgary mountain
But they didn't take me fists so I knocked the jailer down
And bid myself adieu to the jail in Sligo town.
Mush-a-ring-um dur-um dah ...

Now some get their delight in the boxing and the bowling
And some get their delight in the hurling and the rolling
But I gets my delight from the juice of the barley
And courting pretty girls in the morning so early.
Mush-a-ring-um dur-um dah ...

Arrangement © 1995 International Music Publications Ltd, London W6 8BS.
Reproduced by permission. All rights reserved.

Killarney

Words and music by M. W. Balfe

By Kil-lar - ney's lakes and fells, Em - erald Isle and wind-ing bays,
Moun - tain paths and wood-land dells, Mem' - ry ev - er fond - ly strays,
Boun - teous nat - ure loves all lands, Beau - ty wan - ders
ev - 'ry - where Foot - prints leave on ma - ny strands But her home is
sure - ly there. An - gels fold their wings and rest In that Ed - en of the West;
Beau - ty's home, Kil - lar - ney, Heav - 'ns re - flex Kil - lar - ney.

Innisfallen's ruined shrine
May suggest a passing sigh,
But man's faith can ne'er decline
Such God's wonders floating by.
Castle Lough and Glena Bay,
Mountains Tore and Eagle's Nest,
Still at Muckcross you must pray,
Though the monks are now at rest.
Angels wonders not that man
There would fain prolong life's span,
Beauty's home, Killarney,
Ever fair Killarney.

No place else can charm the eye
With such bright and varied tints;
Ev'ry rock that you pass by,
Verdure 'broiders or besprints.
Virgin there the green grass grows,
Ev'ry morn springs natal day,
Bright hued berries daff the snows,
Smiling winter's frown away.
Angels often passing there
Doubt if Eden were more fair,
Beauty's home, Killarney,
Ever fair Killarney.

Music there for echo dwells,
Makes each sound a harmony;
Many-voiced the chorus swells,
Till it faints in ecstasy.
With the charmful tints below,
Seems the heaven above to vie,
All rich colours that we know
Tinge the cloud wreaths in that sky.
Wings of angels so might shine,
Glancing back soft light divine,
Beauty's home, Killarney,
Ever fair Killarney.

The Last Rose of Summer

Words by Thomas Moore, music by R. A. Millikin

'Tis the last rose of summer Left blooming alone, All her lovely companions Are faded and gone! No flow'r of her kindred, No rose bud is nigh, To reflect back her blushes Or give sigh for sigh.

I'll not leave thee, thou lone one,
To pine on the stem;
Since the lovely are sleeping,
Go, sleep thou with them;
Thus fondly I scatter
Thy leaves o'er the bed,
Where thy mates of the garden
Lie scentless and dead.

So soon may I follow,
When friendships decay,
And from love's shining circle
The gems drop away!
When true hearts lie wither'd,
And fond ones are flown,
Oh! who would inhabit
This bleak world alone?

Let Erin Remember the Days of Old

Words by Thomas Moore

Let Erin remember the days of old, Ere her faithless sons betray'd her; When Malachi wore the collar of gold, which he won from the proud invader; When her Kings, with standards of green unfurl'd Led the Red Branch knights to danger; Ere the em-'rald gem of the western world, Was set in the crown of a stranger.

On Lough Neagh's bank as the fisherman strays,
When the clear, cold eve's declining,
He sees the round towers of other days,
In the wave beneath him shining!
Thus shall mem'ry often, in dreams sublime,
Catch a glimpse of the days that are over.
Thus, sighing, look through the waves of time
For the long faded glories they cover!

The Low Backed Car

Traditional folksong
Words by Samuel Lover

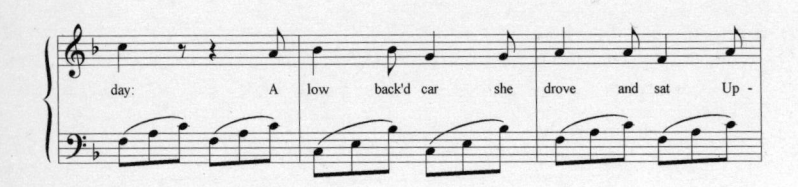

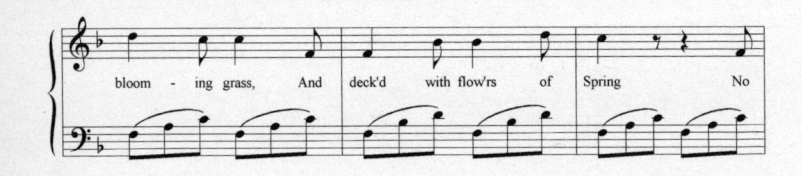

When first I saw sweet Peg-gy, 'Twas on a mar-ket day: A low back'd car she drove and sat Up-on a truss of hay: But when that hay was bloom-ing grass, And deck'd with flow'rs of Spring No flow'r was there, that could com-pare,— To the bloom-ing girl I

The Low Backed Car

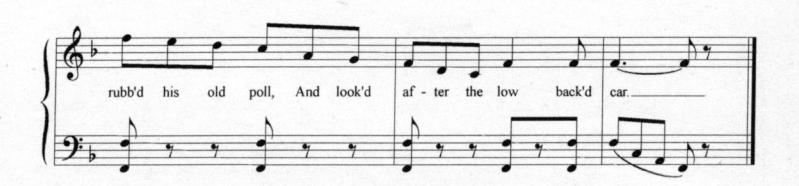

sing, As she sat in her low back'd car, The man at the turn-pike bar, Never as'd for the toll, But just rubb'd his old poll, And look'd after the low back'd car.

In battle's wide commotion,
The proud and mighty Mars,
With hostile scythes demands his tithes
Of death in warlike cars.
But Peggy, peaceful goddess,
Has darts in her bright eye
That knock men down in the market town,
As right and left they fly;
While she sits in her low backed car,
Than battle more dang'rous far,
For the doctor's art cannot cure the heart
That is hit from the low backed car.

The Meeting of the Waters

Traditional
Words by Thomas Moore

There is not in the wide world a val - ley so sweet, As the vale in whose bo - som the bright wa - ters meet, Oh! the last rays of feel - ing and life must de - part Ere the bloom of that val - ley shall fade from my heart, Ere the bloom of that val - ley shall fade from my heart.

The Meeting of the Waters

Yet it was not that nature had shed o'er the scene
Her purest of crystal and brightest of green;
'Twas not her soft magic of streamlet or hill
Oh! no – it was something more exquisite still,
Oh! no – it was something more exquisite still.

'Twas that friends, the belov'd of my bosom, were near,
Who made every dear scene of enchantment more dear,
And who felt how the best charms of nature improve,
When we see them reflected from looks that we love,
When we see them reflected from looks that we love.

Sweet vale of Avoca! how calm could I rest
In thy bosom of shade with friends I love best,
Where the storms that we feel in this cold world should cease,
And our hearts, like thy waters, be mingled in peace,
And our hearts, like thy waters, be mingled in peace.

The Minstrel Boy

Traditional
Words by Thomas Moore

The minstrel boy to the war is gone, In the ranks of death you'll find him; His father's sword he has girded on, And his wild harp slung behind him. "Land of Song!" said the warrior bard, "Tho' all the world betrays thee, One sword, at least thy rights shall guard, One faithful heart shall praise thee."

The minstrel fell! but the foeman's chain
Could not bring that proud soul under;
The harp he lov'd ne'er spoke again,
For he tore its cords asunder,
And said, "No chain shall sully thee,
Thou soul of love and bravery!
Thy songs were made for the pure and free,
They ne'er shall sound in slavery!"

The minstrel boy will return, we pray;
When we hear the news we all will cheer it.
The minstrel boy will return one day,
Torn perhaps in body, not in spirit.
Then may he play on his harp in peace
In a world such as Heav'n intended,
For all the bitterness of man must cease
And ev'ry battle must be ended.

Molly Bawn

Words and music by Samuel Lover

Oh Mol-ly Bawn, why leave me pi-ning, All lone-ly wai-ting here for you? While the stars a-bove are bright-ly shi-ning Be-cause they've no-thing else to do. The flow-ers late were o-pen keep-ing To try a ri-val blush with you, But their mo-ther, Na-ture, set them sleep-ing, With their ro-sy fa-ces wash'd with

Molly Bawn

dew. Oh! Mol-ly Bawn, why leave me pi-ning, All lone-ly wait-ing here for you? The stars a-bove are sweet-ly shin-ing Be-cause they've no-thing else to do, Mol-ly Bawn, Mol-ly Bawn.

Now the pretty flow'rs were made to bloom, dear,
And the pretty stars were made to shine;
And the pretty girls were made for the boys, dear,
And maybe you were made for mine.
The wicked watch dog here is snarling,
He takes me for a thief you see,
For he knows I'd steal you Molly darling
And then transported I should be.

Oh! Molly Bawn, why leave me pining,
All lonely waiting here for you?
The stars above are brightly shining,
Because they've nothing else to do.
Molly Bawn, Molly Bawn!

Molly Brannigan

Traditional

Ma'am dear, did ye ne-ver hear of pret-ty Mol-ly Bran-ni-gan? In troth___ then, she's left me, and I'll ne-ver be a man a-gain. Not a spot on my hide will a sum-mer's sun e'er tan a-gain, since Mol-ly's gone and left me here a-lone for to die. The place where my heart was, you'd ai-sy roll a tur-nip in, 'Tis as

Molly Brannigan

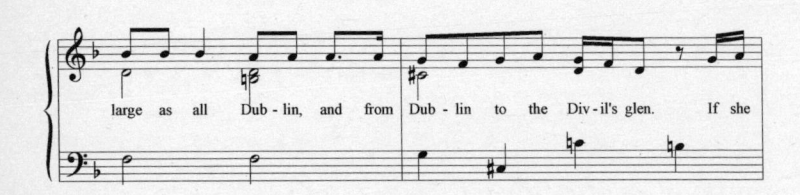

large as all Dublin, and from Dublin to the Divil's glen. If she wished to take another, sure she might have left mine back again, And not have gone and left me here alone for to die.

Ma'am dear, I remember when milking time was past and gone
We strolled through the meadow and she swore I was the only one
That ever she could love, but oh! The base and cruel one
For all that she's left me here alone for to die.

The place where my heart was, you'd aisy roll a turnip in,
'Tis as large as all Dublin, and from Dublin to the Divil's glen,
If she wished to take another sure he might have left mine back again
And not have gone and left me here alone for to die.

Ma'am dear, I remember when coming home the rain began
I wrapt my frieze-coat round her and ne'er a waistcoat had I on
And my shirt was rather fine drawn, but oh! the false and cruel one
For all that she's left me here alone for to die.
The place where my heart was ...

Molly Brannigan

The left side of my carcase is as weak as water gruel, Ma'am.
There's not a pick upon my bones since Molly's proved so cruel, Ma'am.
Oh! if I had a blunder gun I'd go and fight a duel, Ma'am,
For sure I'd better shoot myself that live here to die.
The place where my heart was ...

I'm cool and determined as any salamander, Ma'am.
Won't you come to my wake when I go the long meander, Ma'am?
I'll think myself as valiant as the famous Alexander, Ma'am
When I hear ye crying o'er me, "Arraah! Why did ye die?"
The place where my heart was ...

Arrangement © 1995 International Music Publications Ltd, London W6 8BS.
Reproduced by Permission. All rights reserved.

The Mountains of Mourne

Words and music by Percy French and Houston Collisson

Oh Mary, this London's a wonderful sight, With the people here workin' by day and by night. They don't sow potatoes nor barley nor wheat, But there's gangs o' them diggin' for gold in the street. At least when I ask'd them that's what I was told, So I

© Copyright 1997 Dorsey Brothers Music Limited, 8/9 Frith Street, London W1D 3JB.
All rights reserved. International Copyright secured. Reproduced by permission.

The Mountains of Mourne

just took a hand at this diggin' for gold, But for all that I found there I might as well be where the mountains of Mourne sweep down to the sea.

I believe that when writin' a wish you expressed
As to how the fine ladies in London were dressed.
Well, if you'll believe me, when axed to a ball
They don't wear a top to their dresses at all.
Oh I've seen them myself and you couldn't in thrath
Say if they were bound for a ball or a bath.
Don't be startin' them fashions now Mary Machree
Where the mountains of Mourne sweep down to the sea.

Oft, in the Stilly Night

Traditional
Words by Thomas Moore

Oft, in the stil-ly night, Ere slumber's chain has bound me, Fond mem-'ry brings the light of oth-er days a-round me. The smiles, the tears of boy-hood's years, The words of love then spo-ken; The eyes that shone now dimm'd and gone, The cheer-ful hearts now bro-ken.

Oft in the stil-ly night, Ere slum-ber's chain-has bound me, Fond mem-'ry brings the light of oth-er days a-round me.

Oft, in the Stilly Night

When I remember all
The friends, so linked together,
I've seen around me fall,
Like leaves in wintry weather,
I feel like one who treads alone
Some banquet hall deserted;
Whose lights are fled,
Whose garlands dead,
And all but he departed!
Thus, in the stilly night,
Ere slumber's chain has bound me,
Sad mem'ry brings the light
Of other days around me.

Rory O'More

Words and music by Samuel Lover

Young Rory O'more courted Kathleen Bawn, He was bold as a hawk She as soft as the dawn; He wish'd in his heart pretty Kathleen to please, And he thought the best way to do that was to tease. "Now Rory be aisy," sweet Kathleen would cry, Reproof on her lip but a smile in her eye; "With your tricks I don't know, in truth, what I'm about, Faith you've teas'd till I've put on my coat inside out." "Och jewel," says Rory, "That

Rory O'More

[music: same is the way You've thra-ted my heart for this ma-ny a day, And 'tis pleas'd that I am, and why not, to be sure? For 'tis all for good luck," says bold Ro-ry O' More.]

"Indeed then," says Kathleen, "don't think of the like,
For I half gave a promise to soothering Mike.
The ground that I walk on he loves, I'll be bound."
"Faith," says Rory, "I'd rather love you than the ground."
"Now Rory, I'll cry if you don't let me go,
Sure I dream ev'ry night that I'm hating you so!"
"Oh," says Rory, "that same I'm delighted to hear,
For dreams always go by contrairies my dear.
O Jewel, keep dreaming that same till you die,
And bright morning will give dirty night the black lie.
And 'tis pleas'd that I am and why not to be sure?
Since 'tis all for good luck," says bold Rory O'More.

"Arrah Kathleen, my darling, you've teas'd me enough,
And I've thrash'd for your sake Dinny Grimes and Jim Duff.
And I've made myself, drinking your health, quite a baste,
So I think after that I may to talk to the Priest."
Then Rory the rogue stole his arm round her neck,
So soft and so white without freckle or speck.
And he look'd in her eyes that were beaming with light,
And he kiss'd her sweet lips, don't you think he was right?
"Now Rory, leave off, sir, you'll hug me no more,
That's eight times today that you've kiss'd me before."
"Then here goes another," says he, "to make sure,
For there's luck in odd numbers," says Rory O'More.

The Rose of Tralee

Words by C. Mordaunt Spencer, music by Charles W. Glover

The pale moon was rising above the green mountain, The sun was declining beneath the blue sea; When I stray'd with my love to the pure crystal fountain That stands in the beautiful vale of Tralee: She was lovely and fair, As the rose of the summer, Yet

The Rose of Tralee

'twas not her beauty alone that won me, Oh no, 'twas the truth in her eye ever dawning, That made me love Mary, the Rose of Tralee.

The cool shades of ev'ning their mantle were spreading,
And Mary, all smiling, was list'ning to me,
The moon thro' the valley her pale rays was shedding
When I won the heart of the Rose of Tralee:
Tho' lovely and fair as the rose of the summer,
Yet 'twas not her beauty alone that won me,
Oh, no! 'twas the truth in her eye ever beaming
That made me love Mary, the Rose of Tralee.

She Moved Through the Fair

Traditional

My young love said to me, "My mother won't mind, And my father won't slight you For your lack of kind." And she stepped away from me, And this she did say, "It will not be long, love, Till our wedding day."

She stepped away from me
And went through the fair
And fondly I watched her
Move here and move there
And when she went homeward
With one star awake
As a swan in the evening
Moves over the lake.

Arrangement © 1995 International Music Publications Ltd, London W6 8BS.
Reproduced by permission. All rights reserved.

She Moved Through the Fair

The people were saying
No two were e'er wed
But one had a sorrow
That never was said
And I smiled as she passed
With her goods and her gear
And that was the last
That I saw of my dear.

Last night she came to me,
She came softly in,
So softly she came
That her feet made no din
And she laid her hand on me
And this she did say,
"It will not be long love
Till our wedding day."

Silent, O Moyle

Words by Thomas Moore

Si - lent, o Moyle, be the roar of thy wa - ter, Break not, ye breez - es, your chain of re - pose; While mur - mur - ing mourn - ful - ly, Lir's lone - ly daugh - ter Tells to the night star her tale of woes. When shall the swan, her death note sing - ing, Sleep, with wings in dark ness furl'd? When will Heav'n, its sweet bells ring ing, Call my spi - rit from this storm - y world?

Silent O! Moyle

Sadly, o Moyle, to thy winter-wae weeping,
Fate bids me languish long ages away;
Yet still in her darkness doth Erin lie sleeping,
Still doth the pure light its dawning delay.
When will that day-star, mildly springing,
Warm our isle with peace and love?
When will Heav'n, its sweet bells ringing,
Call my spirit to the fields above?

Sing, Sweet Harp

Words by Thomas Moore

Sing, sweet Harp, oh sing to me Some song of ancient days, Whose sounds, in this sad memory, Long buried dreams shall raise; Some lay that tells of vanish'd fame, Whose light once round us shone, Of noble pride, now turn'd to shame, And hopes for ever gone. Sing, sing, sad Harp, thus sing to me, A-

Sing, Sweet Harp

[music: like our doom is cast, Both lost to all but mem-o-ry, We live but in the past.]

How mournfully the midnight air
    Among thy chords doth sigh,
As if it sought some echo there
    Of voices long gone by;
Of Chieftains, now forgot, who seemed
    The foremost then in fame;
Of Bards, who, once immortal deemed,
    Now sleep without a name.
In vain, sad Harp, the midnight air
    Among thy chords doth sigh,
In vain it seeks an echo there
    Of voices long gone by.

Could'st thou but call those spirits round,
    Who once, in bow'r and hall,
Sat listening to thy magic sound,
    Now mute and mouldering all;
But, no; they would but wake to weep
    The children's slavery;
Then leave them in their dreamless sleep,
    The dead at least are free!
Hush, hush, sad Harp, that dreary tone,
    That knell of Freedom's day;
Or, listening to its death-like moan,
    Let me, too, die away.

Slievenamon

Traditional

All a-lone, all a-lone, by the sea-wash'd shore, All a-lone in the fes-tive hall, The great hall is gay, While the huge waves roar, But my heart is not there at all. It flies far a-way, By the night and the day, To the time and the joys that are gone, I ne-ver shall for-get The sweet maid-en I met In the

It was not the grace of her queenly air,
Nor her cheek of the roses' glow,
Nor her soft black eyes,
Nor her flowing hair,
Nor was it her lily-white brow.
'Twas the soul of truth
And of melting ruth,
And the smile of summer's dawn,
That stole my heart away,
One mild summer day
In the valley near Slievenamon.

In the festive hall, by the star-watched shore,
My restless spirit cries,
"My love, oh my love,
Shall I ne'er see you more,
And my land will you e'er uprise?"
By night and by day
I ever, ever pray,
While lonely my life flows on.
To our flag unrolled
And my true love to unfold
In the valley of Slievenamon.

The Snowy-Breasted Pearl

Traditional

There's a Col-leen fair as May, For a year and for a day I have sought by ev-'ry way her heart to gain. There's no art of tongue or eye Fond youths with maid-ens try, But I've tried with cease-less sigh yet tried in vain. If to France or far-off Spain She'd cross the wat-'ry main, To see her face a-gain the seas I'd brave, And if 'tis heav'n's de-cree That mine she may not be, May the Son of Mar-y me in mer-cy save.

The Snowy-Breasted Pearl

Oh thou blooming milk-white dove,
To whom I've given true love,
Do not ever thus reprove my constancy;
There are maidens would be mine
With wealth in land and kine,
If my heart would but incline to turn from thee.
But a kiss with welcome bland
And touch of thy fair hand
Are all that I demand, wouldst thou not spurn;
For if not mine dear girl
Oh snowy-breasted pearl,
May I never from the fair with life return!

The Spinning Wheel

Traditional
Words by John F Waller

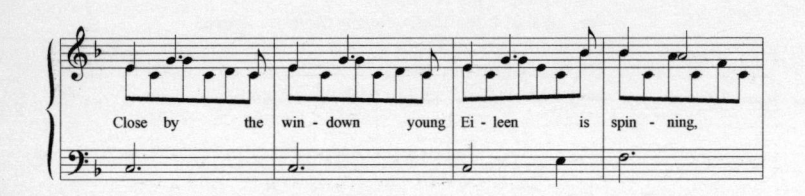

Mellow the moonlight to shine is beginning,
Close by the windown young Eileen is spinning,
Bent o'er the fire her blind grandmother sitting,
Crooning and moaning and drowsily knitting.

CHORUS
Merrily, cheerily, noiselessly whirring,

The Spinning Wheel

Spins the wheel, rings the reel, while the foot's stirring;
Sprightly, and lightly, and airily ringing,
Trills the sweet voice of the young maiden singing.

"What's that noise that I hear at the window, I wonder?"
"'Tis the little birds chirping the holly-bush under."
"What makes you be shoving and moving your stool on,
And singing, all wrong, that old song of 'The Coolun'?"

Merrily, cheerily, noiselessly whirring,
Spins the wheel, rings the reel, while the foot's stirring;
Sprightly, and lightly, and airlily ringing,
Trills the sweet voice of the young maiden singing.

There's a form at the casement, the form of her true love,
And he whispers with face bent: 'I'm waiting for you, love;
Get up from the stool, through the lattice step lightly,
We'll rove in the grove while the moon's shining brightly.'

Merrily, cheerily, noiselessly whirring...

The Spinning Wheel

The maid shakes her head, on her lips lays her fingers,
Steals up from the stool – longs to go, and yet lingers;
A frightened glance turns to her drowsy grandmother,
Puts one foot on the stool, spins the wheel with the other.

Merrily, cheerily, noiselessly whirring...

Lazily, easily, swings now the wheel round,
Slowly and lowly is heard now the reel's sound;
Noiseless and light to the lattice above her,
The maid steps – then leaps to the arms of her lover.

Slower and slower and slower the wheel swings;
Lower and lower and lower the reel rings;
Ere the reel and the wheel stop their ringing and moving,
Through the grove the young lovers by moonlight are roving.

The Star of the County Down

Traditional
Words by Cathal McGarvey

Near to Ban-bridge Town in the Coun-ty Down On a morn-ing in Ju-ly, Down a bo-reen green came a sweet col-leen And she smiled as she passed me by. Oh! she looked so sweet, from her two white feet To the sheen of her nut-brown hair, Such a

CHORUS

coax-in' elf, I'd to shake my-self, To make sure I was real-ly there. Oh from Ban-try Bay up to Der-ry Quay, And from Gal-way to Dub-lin town, No

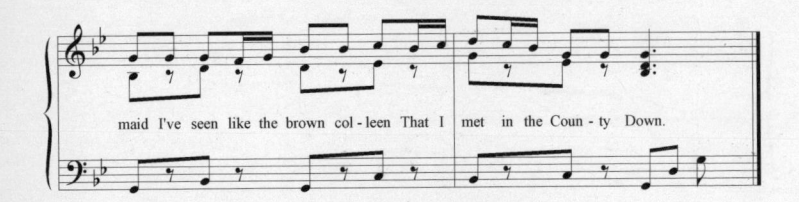

The Star of the County Down

maid I've seen like the brown colleen That I met in the County Down.

As she onward sped I scratched my head
And I gazed with a feelin' quare,
There I said, says I, to a passer-by,
"Who's the maid with the nut-brown hair?"
Oh! he smiled at me, and with pride says he,
"That's the gem of Ireland's crown,
Young Rosie McCann, from the banks of the Bann,
She's the star of the County Down."

Oh! from Bantry Bay up to Derry Quay,
And from Galway to Dublin town,
No maid I've seen like the brown colleen
That I met in the County Down.

At the harvest fair she'll surely be there,
So I'll dress in my Sunday clothes,
And I'll try sheep's eyes and deludtherin lies,
On the heart of the nut-brown Rose.
No pipe I'll smoke, no horse I'll yoke,
Tho' my plough with rust turn brown,
Till a smiling bride by my own fireside
Sits the star of the County Down.

Oh! from Bantry Bay up to Derry Quay,
And from Galway to Dublin town,
No maid I've seen like the brown colleen
That I met in the County Down.

Teddy O'Neale

Traditional

I've come to the cab-in, he danc'd his wild jigs in, As neat a mud pa-lace as ev-er was seen and con-sid-'ring it serv'd to keep poul-try and pigs in, I'm sure it was al-ways most el-e-gant clean! But now, all a-bout it seems lone-ly and drea-ry, All sad and all si-lent, no pi-per, no reel; Not ev-en the sun thro' the case-ment is cheer-y, Since I miss the dear dar-ling boy, Ted-dy O' Neale.

Teddy O'Neale

I dreamt but last night, (oh! bad luck to my dreaming,
I'd die if I thought 'twould come surely to pass.)
But I dreamt, while the tears down my pillow were
   streaming,
That Teddy was courtin' another fair lass.
Och! did not I wake with a weeping and wailing,
The grief of that thought was too deep to conceal;
My mother cried: Norah, child, what is your ailing?:
And all I could utter was "Teddy O'Neale."

Shall I ever forget, when the big ship was ready
The moment had come, when my love must depart,
How I sobbed like a spalpeen, "Goodbye to you Teddy,"
With drops on my cheek and a stone at my heart.
He says 'tis to better his fortune he's roving,
But what would be gold, to the joy I would feel
If I saw him come back to me, honest and loving
Still poor, but my own darling Teddy O'Neale.

There's a Heart in Old Ireland

Traditional

Oh! the day bright and clear, and the sky deep-est blue, And my thoughts turn back to a heart fond and true There's a dear lit-tle cab-in far o-ver the sea Where some-one is anx-ious-ly wait-ing for me. There's a heart in old Ire-land that's pi-ning for

There's a Heart in Old Ireland

(me,) And there's "Two Irish eyes", that gaze out on the sea, But I'll soon be returning and once again be, With the heart in old Ireland that's pining for me.

Oh! in fancy I see my old Ireland so dear,
And the Lakes of Killarney so lovely and clear,
I can see the old Shannon flow down to the sea,
Where I first met the heart that is pining for me.

There's a heart in old Ireland that's pining for me,
And there's ,"Two Irish Eyes", that gaze out on the sea,
But I'll soon be returning and once again be,
With the heart in old Ireland that's pining for me.

The Wearin' o' the Green

Traditional

Oh!— Pad-dy dear, an' did you hear the news that's go-in' round? The Sham-rock is for-bid by law to grow on I-rish ground! St Pat-rick's day no more we'll keep, his co-lour can't be seen, For there's a cru-el law a-gin the wea-rin' o' the green! I met wi' Nap-per Tan-dy an' he took me by the hand An' he said "How's poor ould Ire-land, an' how does she stand?" She's the

The Wearin o the Green

...most distressful country that ever yet was seen, For they're hangin' men and women there for wearin' o' the green.

She's the most distressful country that ever yet was seen, For they're hangin' men and women there for wearin' o' the green.

Then since the colour we must wear is England's cruel red,
Sure Ireland's sons will ne'er forget the blood that they have shed;
You may pull the shamrock from your hat, and cast it on the sod,
But 'twill take root and flourish there, tho' underfoot 'tis trod!
When laws can stop the blades of grass from growin' as they grow,
And when the leaves in summertime their verdure dare not show,
Then I will change the colour too, I wear in my caubeen,
But till that day, please God! I'll stick to wearin' o' the green!

She's the most distressful country that ever yet was seen,
For they're hangin' men and women there for wearin' o' the green.

The Wearin' o' the Green

But if at last our colour should be torn from Ireland's heart,
Her sons, with shame and sorrow, from the dear ould isle will part;
I've heard a whisper of a land that lies beyond the sea,
Where rich and poor stand equal in the light of freedom's day.
Ah! Erin! must we leave you, driven by a tyrant's hand?
Must we seek a mother's blessing from a strange and distant land?
Where the cruel cross of England shall never more be seen,
And where, please God, we'll live and die, still wearin' o' the green!

She's the most distressful country that ever yet was seen,
For they're hangin' men and women there for wearin' o' the green.

Widow Machree

Traditional

Widow Machree, it's no wonder you frown, Och hone! Widow Machree, Faith it ru-ins your looks, that same dirty black gown, Och hone! Widow Machree, How alter'd your air with that close cap you wear, 'Tis destroying your hair which should be flowing free; Be no longer a churl, of its black silken curl, Och hone! Widow Machree.

Widow Machree, now summer is come,
Och hone! Widow Machree;
When everything smiles,
Should a beauty look glum?
Och hone! Widow Machree,
See the birds go in pairs,
And the rabbits and hares,
Why even the bears now in couples agree;
And the mute little fish,
Tho' they can't speak, they wish,
Och hone! Widow Machree.

Widow Machree, and when winter comes in,
Och hone! Widow Machree,
To be poking the fire all alone is a sin,
Och hone! Widow Machree.
Sure, the shovel and tongs,
To each other belongs,
While the kettle sings songs,
Full of family glee;
Yet alone with your cup,
Like a hermit you sup,
Och hone! Widow Machree.

And how do you know,
With the comforts I've told,
Och hone! Widow Machree,
But you're keeping some poor fellow
Out in the cold?
Och hone! Widow Machree.
With such sins on your head,
Sure your peace must be fled,
And you can't sleep in bed,
Without thinking to see
Some ghost or some sprite,
That will wake you each night, crying
Och hone! Widow Machree.

Then take my advice, darling Widow
    Machree,
Och hone! Widow machree;
And with that advice, faith,
I wish you'd take me,
Och hone! Widow Machree.
You'd have me to desire,
Then to stir up the fire,
And, sure, hope is no liar,
In whispering to me.
That the ghosts would depart
When you'd me near your heart,
Och hone! Widow Machree.